Our Hearts Are a Burial Ground

Lesley Belleau

Copyright © 2025 by Lesley Belleau

All rights reserved. No part of this publication may be reproduced or transmitted in any form or by any means, electronic or mechanical, including photocopying, recording or any information storage and retrieval, without the written permission of the publisher. Names, characters, places and incidents are either the product of the author's imagination or used fictitiously, and any resemblance to actual persons living or dead, events or locales is entirely coincidental. All trademarks are properties of their respective owners.

Published by
BookLand Press Inc.
15 Allstate Parkway, Suite 600
Markham, Ontario L3R 5B4
www.booklandpress.com

Printed in Canada

Library and Archives Canada Cataloguing in Publication

Title: Our hearts are a burial ground / Lesley Belleau.
Names: Belleau, Lesley, 1976- author.
Series: Modern Indigenous voices.
Description: Series statement: Modern Indigenous voices
Identifiers: Canadiana (print) 20250243318 | Canadiana (ebook) 2025024411X | ISBN 9781772312553 (softcover) | ISBN 9781772312560 (EPUB)
Subjects: LCGFT: Poetry.
Classification: LCC PS8553.E45698 O97 2025 | DDC C811/.6—dc23

We acknowledge the support of the Government of Canada through the Canada Book Fund. We acknowledge the support of the Canada Council for the Arts. We acknowledge funding support from the Ontario Arts Council and the Government of Ontario.

Table of Contents

She Braids Her Own Hair / Okaadenidizo | 5

Underwater / Anaamiindim | 6

Daanis | 8

Empty Skying / Zhiigonigaade | 9

Lost Sister | 10

Nishime / A Prayer | 11

Baakise | 12

Spiderwebbing | 14

Her Crying | 16

Boodawe | 18

The Eating | 19

Awesiinh | 21

By a Tree / Jiigaag | 23

Window | 24

The Fear | 26

Our Hearts Are a Burial Ground | 28

The Capture / Zaagi'idiwin | 30

Second One | 33

Bianca | 35

Chasing for Too Long | 36

The Glass Children | 37

Bangitoo | 38

Hair Across the Couch | 39

The Swallowing / Gondon | 40

Lost | 42

Home / Apike | 44

Everything Reminds Me of You | 47

Darkness | 49

Guilt Is an Oasis for Truth | 50

He Was Never Here | 52

Sweatlodge | 54

Arms Soldiering | 56

Lichen Skin | 57

Dream of Lost Graveyard | 58

She Braids Her Own Hair / Okaadenidizo

Midnight, no curl to it, a longing.
Every strand is a strangling,
That voice under the water-halo,
mermaid fish, those nibanaabe,
Are hoping that braid divides our rivers.
Full moon hands, black hair shadowing the
Half-pull, the lulling, and winding, the ends
A shadow blanketing genocide.

You are thirteen and your braid is a threat.

Cuspy weavers inside of necessity's dank
Promises. Your fingers are fireflies, they are
Old hymns, they are the tablecloth
That hid our stories.

Your braiding is cutting the numbered voices in threes,
An undiscovered triangular ceremony.
You are rewinding numbers, you are piecing their voices
Into a thick nestling-
And Nikomis says,
"my turn, our hearts are wet with your prophecy."

Underwater / Anaamiindim

Low sounds she dips and curls, braiding with nibi, her sounds a twilight, an echo, that curt nod of memory. Blooksuckers thick, their plucking an imaginary popping under the frayed mass of the river, their dark bodies betrayed.

She is a flight, the river carrying.

Her hands are ten oars fighting off charcoaled Sundays: a decoy, a long braid skimming the surface. She chases the mermaids, the story-dwellers, those pebbled faces that use history as a magnet.

Underwater, it is an orchestra.

Love bones suckling seaweed, old lip memories tracing that bone flight of the river-bottom, the fragment of her grandmother pressing her, her long braid an anchor, pummeling itself into the numbered sand-spaces.

Her mother told her to love in sequence.

Her father showed her the splintered edges of abandonment.

She forgot all stories when the seaweed suctioned her braid around her, not moving, the paralysis of surface hunting, orbs pushing their greedy need in small spectacles above her head.

The intrusion of beavers, frogs, tadpoles, gone. Her mouth opening, ready to inhale sedimentary hope.

She unwraps her hair underwater, her breath a nuisance,
her temples begging for air, all flying things a memory,
no gracing now. Anaamibiig. Goodikwebani'o.

Low sounds, heart forcing itself to rise,
her chin a new mountain.

Oooho ooh oooh oh oh ooh, the silence of shore, her hands
wringing out her braid,

The squish of permanence, a buoy, a dribbling of need, a
thousand sand soldiers created.

Daanis

Beautiful girl bloated by a strong river,
Covered by hidden policies and words shaped,
Edged like ancestral secrets along the shore.

You sang your name once to me,
Told me about hindsight and blasphemy-
Decided to carve yourself to dust
Bit by filament-bit.

That golden thumb hitchhiking pain away
You said you knew that headlight, that inner
sanction, and then you fell inside the broken path
You didn't fall so fast.

Your beauty is a landslide
A sucking of mud, all the sinking in,
Your face is lost
I want to tread into, I want boots, I want hooks
To find you
Claysongs, the side of your cheek is leaning,
A ditch, and our song is corrupting the vacancy
Of petroglyphying promises.

And I sing your song again
You are still falling,
Landslide, you have to find my hands.

Empty Skying / Zhiigonigaade

Leaving the Sky
He leaves. I have never left. Tries to
Return and his offerings are leavings,
Those leaves that flit in the fall, silty.
Every father who left reminds me of you.

You are the wailing sound of September,
You are the offering feast without a table.
Nokomis moves her blanket across the sky, her prelude
is a hand that moves her body over babies, she
Mouths the breath bones, she opens
Her ribcage and creates her babies' stars.
Anang gii-piidagoojin.

In sleep, I know you. In waking, you are the drummer
without strumming, don't look at me-
a key without a door, a baby's mouth searching,
an opened mouth turned to the sky
Zhiigonigaade
A Sky without a name drowns.
The stars forget your name.

Lost Sister

The sister under that white wing,
Struggling, cleft of a last breath- (couldn't hear that last pant.)
There is no reasoning left in this heart,
A butterfly knowing her death is certain.
Lips and promises and hands, an unwinding of prophecy.

Shattering everything at once, my heart is a wing. You ate her.
You gnawed the last drippings, you stalled her only flight.
Trying to land to die is a crooked Tree branch,
breathing a name that only dusk can hear.
The way you say midnight sounds like a fight, your teeth
Are charcoaled white. I found you beside
Love's corner, hunched over, begging.

The dip of your smile a curse.
Remember her laughing over the rolling
Hurt that brought us to this shoreline-
The sand creating your smile is that old bloodsucker
You parted her hair before you kissed her-
you missed the indent
Of her voice, her calling, her body, hiccupping, sleeping stories,
Breath waking new cavings,
those petroglyphs shaking under rock.

Nishime / A Prayer

Pregnant, her writhing in me, her heart a beacon.
I didn't want him to be there the first time I saw her face.
Begging,
Begging, begging, begging, begging, I lost my name.

My heart became a home of caves.
I wanted to lick that sun that forgot me,
Needing that crucible of need,
and there are no corners here, only soft edges,
Like sponges.

I found the hug I always wanted in this place,
curled over me, dark and
Praying for breath. No sleep, no songs, no desire,
more spirit than the span of eyes.
Blank space, no taste, a cauldron of regret
that kills soft bodies
Over and over.
I still remember how to smile when people are watching.
It reminds me of how the late summer
Gives us empty milkweeds. Squeezing and squeezing,
Dreaming their milk on our hands.

Baakise

Yes, the swallowing throat of my name
Before you forgot me.

Wiinzo. All the names. You scream my
Name, you open my name, licking your
Fingers when you drank my memory,
Silvering, all the snowing, so dark.

Trees indented, those birds I counted
Into safety when you choked on
My juices. It's too late, find me here. It's
So dark and you remind me- I can't see the
Shape of you, those curls of night are your hair,
Your wounding made her bow low into hiding.

You pulled my clothes off and the
Swallowed snow melting, pine trees, and
Scentings a thrust, slivers, songs, pressing
Her face and mine.
Zhingobiiwaatig.
I can't see you I can't see you I can't see you
I'm being eaten, windigo trails flailing
The treetops bending
Limbs offering herself, face lit up and arms opened wide.
Booni.

Her garden, petals catching this open,
Emptied body.
Thinking it was nikomis or nibi before
I saw you for the last time. Booni. Your
Opening so splintered, creaking,
Tiptoeing around and around.

A sanctuary of lies; debwewin's lost
Sister. You ate that wing like a promise.

Spiderwebbing

Angering and ditching life through
Each strand, Landing
Imagining that you might come
Back here again.

Webbing might be a prison
Walls a casket, stranding
A fall unlanding, you stop
Unwinding those threads
Those needles we know.

Seedlings, she buries her face.
Braiding them. Three wounding
Braids are sisters cuddling,
But her legs are long, flickering.

Licking the lies of her life
Winding and winding and winding
A tasting of homing; she is
Knitting babies' hats until her fingers bleed.

Stomach tattooing namings, fingers bulbous,
Starlets swirl until Giizi bows,
Hurled like an uncurled anchor
Heaving and heaving a death was like a
New and bursting nest.

Those thousand legs are a future.
My baby pickpocketing my heart-
Yours under hers, your restless sleeping,
The way you turn to your skeleton to think,
Praying down to an unsure sky.

You walk like you are free, a slight bump
That only the horizon might see.
But your eyes have bars that only the moon recognizes.

Tumeric, ginger, the wanting on your breath, that hiss that
Can slay a thousand warriors, maidens, no, me, me, me,
A tea left cold where your hand left it.

I save the memory of you the same way
I pack my babies things
Once they grow, using my heart
like a little box to keep things
Remembered.

A heaving pulse when I wake up to you gone.
Another ghost
Dream where you were there, that smile that reminds me
Of chasing my father's love, entering me the same way a
Family can be slain in the night.

These memories are stairs.
You are the sandcastle I couldn't finish.
You are the first drawing I forgot to name.

Identity threads her name on the art of your face,
You are my open canyon.

Her Crying

Scared she will be kidnapped. Her
Dream catcher behind her bed, and she cut
The side of her face trying to reach for it. Her,
Finding my pillow.

She's alive. I tell her this. Memories and
My palm in hers and her breathing slows. Watching her,
Watching her, watching her, watching her.
Sleep is hard memory.
A kwe finding a bush to hide in. Every pant is a dream.

Grandmother's story is a tree-a branch now,
a twig spread in her palm,
And she's punching. Her stories are a storm,
her body has become
A reason to run, and the back of her throat is an animal,
growling.

So low-
(I remember my mommy humming, drumming somewhere.)
Growling, sasquatching, until memory- it's gone.

There is no truth, is there? He took my- her, all of it, all of us.
Throwing
Up in the bathroom, blood. Ashkode bending and broken,
his wiindigo voice
A song that I scream-a dream death,
palms crushing my name, her mouth open,
Tongue a flag, so red, clay dying inside of firelight.

Aagonwetan. No rest, sleep, crying.
Scratching her hair and face and
Blood music on her pillow.

When she cries, I know who stole her;
Those hands older than drowning, those hands
Sent to eat our children. Except, I'm here watching.

Your hands are a memory, hands swallowed by debwewin.
The Bear Walks. The Bearwalks.
Maakwa.
But the baby bear. Makoons. That innocence.
Let that be your streaming.

Her tears, a long story.
Mine too daanis, mine too.

Boodawe

The tsunami of your smile, eyes
Her laugh, centuries, her body a long
Enclaved side, a face so pulling,
Sand winding our feet,
The only witness,
her long back arching.

(The small indent behind your ear, the urge when you
Reach back, your pull, your ancient stories inside me).

Imagine if my skin unfolds your library.
The center, you find me.
the way that Nikomis holds your face,
The Origin, the cavewalls, your breath,
Imagine if the birth of fire kept
Secrets that made her move in her sleep,
Tiny whelps that helped the trees breathe
In and out, her pant so arrogant
Bizaani-ayaa- a sudden shape of love in the corner.

Boodawe.

The Eating
(For Kevin)

I heard he died drunk on the streets of Ottawa.
These men came and kicked him until all breath was gone.
He was known as a drunk on the streets,
his picture was taken with him lying there,
passed out, his head nodded to the side,
his chest still breathing up and down
up and down.

Feet pressed against his long hair, muddying
it, tangling it against the sidewalk.

The photographer said, "Fucking look at that."
and he bled into himself
being kicked and stomped when he couldn't
defend himself.

I think of his heart scraping the midnight streets,
remembering his family, wailing for the
beast to stop gnawing his heart so bleeding
opened, his crying against the asphalt before
he knelt to blackness.
When we were kids we took the same bus.
Sat together, the wavering bus
steadying itself with each stop.
His same long hair covering his face,
brown skin glimpsing itself
under the afternoon sun,
but he never said a word.
Walking into his long driveway,
hair over his face, walking,
his sister running, his brother

behind him, his daddy at the
front stoop, waiting.
He is our family because we breathed ourselves alive
in the same land
helped each other
but no one was there for him when he was sick,
drowning, choking alone.
We are all hurting. How did we let him suffer alone there,
to drown alone. When we are kicked, and beaten, we choke
on our own blood. We swim in our ancestors' blood, we are not
alone in our blood.
Drowning is solitary. If someone is beside us, the
hope in the long, sustained body, swimming,
legs still kicking, chest pumped, air, the long air
still air in dreaming, no concrete cheekbones,
nibi pulling us and shorelines,
memories, ancestors' fires, the
flicker of a last moonlight,
her old face telling the last story.

Hands pulling up, she is pulling me up, her face above me,
the water pouring out of my lungs like an offering
Screams so far away, earbuds lost, the hope of a
shoreline footbanking,
water from my nose, her hands in my hair,
she came. The dark loom of his memory resisting
in my marrow, his slow walking,
the last time he turned and watched
the bus pull away,
brown eyes begging through his hair.

Minjemendan.

Awesiinh

She falls,
It is all different once the world speaks. bizaan.
gidoombiigiz.
Whisper outside: trails, crooked, followed.
Footprints, the window-edge where love sits
bizaan igo ani-maajidoon.
Can you hear me clearing my heart from you?

Breath in, ojibwemo
Burrowed, easy to crawl inside of,
Vacancy, open a small mouth, every crevice swallowing,
Her hands loosening,
Danwewesin.

We tried to bury her, our little hands so quick,
so bored with each
other, the long-armed trees that knew our names.

Caverns are ravenous, trying to turn the page of a book
That trail, too dark and nobody wants to open her story,
mouth skimming her drippings,
a tongue as wide as the old trails,
Her ear against the pulse of the sand, dug, dug, so new,
She hears the blood before her name scrapes her skin.
Beading, all those old lines, and the palm of your handscape.

Caving, grab my hand over the rocksounds.
A grandmother holds the side of a tent open,
Footprints, the imprint of a stone when you breathe,
awesiinh, The low pant,
Growling, hips swallowing your sound when you
Strain to say my name.

That wind, I still dream I hear you.
Noondagwad: that sound, trees,
the spine straightened, stories,
Look what's in your hand, it's not holding me.
The halfmoon, rustles, her half whimper,
Curling, underwater voices.

Little bones are my pillow,
memory is my blanket.

I walked into your arms. gwayakotam.
She hears the right things. My sisters
Laughing, their long mouths
Not knowing fear.
trees, faces, silence,
sewn into your walk.
That sang our stories for us.

awesiinh. My daddy loved you.
You ate each plate, you sat with him.

awesiinh
We tried to eat each other's footprints.

By a Tree / Jiigaag

Those early mornings with you
Pressed into my back,
The pieces of bark under my
Fingernails, Splinters, teeth yanking
Erect shards of wood,
spitting them on my pantleg,
A fern, its plucking and spilling and
Sharpening, finding new bloodsongs.
So red, lean my chin against history,
Tongue, the sweat and the thigh
Swallowing me.

I hear the ground when I taste you.
I am wondering how deep you can go,
How far, how wide can you spread your
Stories.

Window

Winter coming,
Breath clouds on the window, and
I am naked, so cold, nipples a
Scrape on wood.
Old panes, rattling with whistles
Kissing my neck, cold.

My cheek watching the black shape beside
Daddy's arched tree.
No footprints when you scour the limbs of
Her long hands, her body tense and full of a
Promise.
Snout so sure, tail caressing the pockets
Of her histories.

You must have heard my breathing, that instinct.
Your tail a flag, so slow, sound matching the wind,
Yellowed eyes, rise of neck fur, the way the
Trees bow back.

Not coming closer, your eyes trace the window
Like a baby's new face.
Her sound
Hearing her own howl, feet pressed,
Ground, her legs quivering, she is opening,
The sky, blue pulse, pushing her mouth down.

Long nails cut the trail-line, her eyes search for a clearing.

Aweshiinh, her legs, her front arms bending.
Rustles beside her ear, she wants
A soft mound of leaves,
Chin bedding, the tense crispness of footprints,
she drags herself
Sideways, chewing, chewing, the earth in her mouth,
no sound.

Not her first birth, she tries to stand.
Opening burning, so hot, she thinks she's breaking,
Eyes finding a birch tree, tracing her sound, her long
Song downwards.

Someone travelling, her breath, the burn,
The memory of a radiant sun, being chased, swallowing
The lakewater, drowning,
Her body is moving, can't breathe
Until the undersound of fur pressing into winter and
Red red over snow, a mother's soft lapping.

ondaadizike.

The Fear

Coming after every daughter
Thinking every morning is the last time.

No walking to school alone
The them how to use keys,
How to stab someone in the throat.

The praying- it's a constancy. The
Begging, so much begging.

Not sleeping ever, watching small
Hearts under pajamas.
History has wound our laughter and bedtimes,
Mornings and the sleeping. Every doorframe
Feels like a way into the house, the heart,
This pulse, this shoulder that denies
Your entrance is a wound.
Every lock is a promise.

The mailmain is suspect. The guy who bumps
Me with the cart in a grocery store. That
Knock on the door by my Purolator. I lock
Down the house, and I carry my daughters
Into safety. So fast.

Burrowed under blankets. That side of a lamp
That I unplugged just in case. Waiting for
The shards of the door to spray on our faces.

I am forty-five and I still can't breathe if someone
Knocks on my door. No sleeping.

Ask their fathers why. The same way
I'm asking mine.

Our Hearts Are a Burial Ground

Fingernails ripped off, dirt slinging, grave searching,
A silence of memory, babywatching, bodywatching,
The doors that never keep death out.
Death records and birth records yellowing
In our closets, little clothes falling apart.

Songs we sing in our sleep and wake up
Halfway through like we were
Being awakened by a gravekeeper.
Those nights and tears remembering,
Not wanting to know what they did to our babies.
Names were ignored. We know their names.

Every single one had a name.
If they didn't get a chance, then
The burial ground will open,
And their names will crawl outside the
Ground into history's arrogant heart.

Wanisin   Abinoojinyens.
Bones a thousand years old, still waiting for us.

Sticks.
Sticks in her hand, her small hand walking forward
All her fervor, all her weight, hitting him in the head,
She never stops hitting in the head.
Five years old and she wants to hurt everything.
That beaver fled, her head dipped underwater, her tail flapped once.

I told her not to hit her.
She was wading in the water, peace was there.
She disappeared, she discovered the underwater,
And my daughter laughed and ran,
A lone stick in my hand, reddening the water,
A long cut, running after her,
Trails of wounded flowers her footpath.

The Capture / Zaagi'idiwin

Memory, the ladder, and slipping on each rung, ears ringing.

It's September again, and I want to cry. I want a shoulder to open beside me, to slip down on like an avalanche. A mudslide, my face screaming over history, quick and downward.

The uncoloured leaves bring me backwards, bangishin. The smells are ancient hands pulling me backwards. Aazhigijishin. Backwards, spiralled, and I am bare in a bloodsucker lake, my sisters and daddy pulling them off my chest, stomach, legs.

Waking up panting, the sweat on my sheets, pillows, my heart pounding like a hard rainfall.

I look over and my baby is still sleeping. My dreams are my own, cemented into my own skin, and I see the colour of her peace on her face, so perfect.

I move over, wondering why the walls sometimes look so foreign and dreaming seems more familiar. I move closer to her, wanting her breath to become a reminder of this day, this minute, to stop the remembering, to stop the years from closing in. I go back to sleep inside of her breathing, that steady in and out that is like climbing, feet digging in hardened clay, reddened, one step at a time.

The kids wake up like a clanging, mouths moving floorboards, curtains, the footsteps, hands opening cupboards, laughing, bums on cushions bouncing, the living, all that living forcing my eyes open. Hungover, groggy, I pull the blankets backwards.

Aazhigijishin. *She is falling backwards.* Aazhigijishin. Bloodsuckers pulling me onto shore, a whole river of them, forcing my eyes open, no one to pull them off, skinned red as ochre, I force my feet on my cold laminate floor, head pounding. I look forward smiling, hands reaching for frypans, eggs, instant coffee, and little morning hands, warm to the touch.

When they are in school, I look at the imprints their heads left on the pillows and wonder where time edged away to and hear one of my Daddy's trees falling behind my old house, and I hold onto the counter as hard as I can, knuckles whitened, fingerpads pressed, pressing, pressing. gawa'igaazo.

The crunch of the tree hitting the ground. She fell, and I looked at the rungs of her history laid bare, so naked. I lay down on the bunkbed and inhale over and over, as if that would suck back time into our bodies. Her branches gasping, our woodstove crackling my childhood awake.

When my body was a map of bruises, we climbed. We were ten hands hanging from branches, no ladder to climb down from. The scrape of bark tattooing us as we fell. onjibizo. There was no water, but we saw the orbing of nibi over and over for years, shoring us. The treebranch held her hand, her gnarled fingers coming out from the ground, pulling us out, safe. We still watch for her in every squirrel pathway, in every tree my children climb.

September and legs running home from school, backpacks like turtle's shells, bouncing. I watch their faces, wondering how they learned to hold the glint of sun in their eyes when they run, the scent of leaves when they push open the door. One of my daughters asked me *Mama, is it okay to laugh when you feel like crying or cry when you feel like laughing?* Her eyes pulling pulling like the first time she looked up at me after birth, a thousand years old.

Why baby why baby why baby why? Thinking something happened at school. *You didn't answer my question.*

Her eyes circling mine over and over, her mark on my heart ringing it ringing it with fear and love. My mother doing our laundry in the sink looking out the window, saying nothing. *What do you think?* Her pearl-tanned skin a memory of riverbeds. *A question for a question, right?*

And she was up the stairs and the question hung, fell, bounced, my hand on the banister, knowing I missed her need because her question scared me. Letting her go without chasing her, bending down to my other children asking how their day was. The edge of regret sits so close to knowing, deep breaths always a suction.

Afraid to fall, that cliff-edge near, the quicksand mountain and those rocks with heartbeats holding me up.

Second One

Leaving a Mountain
Awasajiw.
The blonde baby that surprised us, like I did. Except without the grandfather that kept asking my father- "Is she one of us- is he one of us?" He didn't have to be ashamed of his white-blonde hair and blue eyes. I blocked that- like a kick to the lungs. No one will hurt him.

All those rolls in his legs I washed that tickled him. His laugh was a verse from a book of promises. And his sleeping became fearful- I watched watched watched- so afraid that something would happen. his tossing was an entire creation reborn. So grateful.

My baby. Chubby hands always ready to cup my cheeks when he saw his father hurt me. Curling around him like the moon and talking in that ear while he clutched his favorite patchwork blanket that he fell in love with at a garage sale. "It's ok- I'm here- I will never leave." He took his blanket one night and pushed it against my cheeks, not saying anything. Just kept wiping the tears, over and over. That was one of the biggest gifts that I've ever had. And I knew he was a mountain that moment.

His eyes knew the world faster than me. He drew everything in. People, objects, water, the sky- he wanted everything. It was so hard watching him because of the harsh beauty that he crawled on.

The fear prayers are a cross country race, and we are panting, heaving, breathing, inhaling dirt. So fast, everything's leaving. Everyone loved him- a reserve filled with dark haired boys and his blue eyes kicking. So scared when he hated kindergarten- his first day- clutching on my leg, sobbing- begging me not to leave him. I remember picking his fingers off me one by one trying to explain that it had to happen- you have to go. The blue eyes staring at me, so hurt, when I walked away, his screaming. My back against the school wall, weeping, needing to run back and save him. Hating the world- not wanting to leave my baby. Being made to leave my baby. Curled in my bed, waiting for him to come home.

He is a silent flooding. Protected by a hood of flat mushrooms. Four years old and knowing the way home. Flooding the kindergarten floor, their prying their way in through the doors. And his smile and run when I came to get him, his feet wet, all the other children watching. Into my arms, kissing my cheeks and hair.

We walked home, his hand in mine, and we talked about making biscuits, and how footsteps look, and he ran and tried to reach a tall treebranch- yelling at me to "get it mommy- you are so tall- get it," and I did. His hands were over those leaves like they were a piece of heaven. We went into our small apartment, and we made dinosaurs out of cheese, and he asked me, tears, tears, "Why did you leave me there. You said you would never leave."

Those red numbed claw marks staining the base of the mountains our hands still clawing at the base.

Bianca

I have never written a poem about you.

That windy creek lost between your sisters.
Because you seemed strong enough
to take this world on and mine
And I didn't realize that you weren't.
Every move now so tentative, I should have pushed,
pushed and pushed your voice.
gaanda'amaw.

You aren't a shard, no glass, no shadow,
no shallow-spliced
Ripple, no rope that holds an anchor, no frame around a
Picture, no echo, no echo, no echo. Not shattered.

Golden-spining,
That rainbow-colour that can't be named.

You came from me screaming,
the loudest cry I have ever heard:
Black hair, fingers and toes curled and purpled,
the rapture of the
World touching your skin for the first time.

You are the mermaid that makes memory afraid to lift her
arrogant head.
You are the current that nibi loosens her power-dreams for.
You are the waking moment from dream to knowing this
heavy earth.
You are the one that holds my hand.

Wars are started and ended with hearts like yours.

Chasing for Too Long

Zip-tied, gagged.
Bizaan-ayaa. Giishkowe.
Hands bound, no tongue, the saliva
a taunting.
All these ghosts with guitars
Singing our namings, our birthsongs.
Wandering our pathways for us.
Our children are umbilical tattoos,
Invisible bellybuttons,
Heirloom footmarks.

Their hurts bend backs,
Makes us scour streets, turn our
hearts into hunters.

Long tremors that the beavers
Can't chase.
Don't become invisible, daanis.

The Glass Children

My second and third daughters get
Tired of being the second and third daughters.

Always lost inside of chasing their sister.
Always coming along for the ride,
A long song that isn't theirs.

Long hair, we are so lost inside of each other,
Building temples that keep falling,
Our limbs braiding and braiding, and trying to
Rewind the braiding, until our knuckles are
Knotted. Roped.

Hugging is taken by the windigo,
Our steps are a pardon, a formation of marks
Begging, our eyes are begging.
We hug over each other's shoulders, we move forward
With permission. We hold each other's hands in secret.

Mama- they ask, *make her stop.*
That quicksand where they fall into, my hand
Pulling them up over and over, but after hers,
A temple destroyed, a child degrading a
Permanence.

A cure that looks through stained glass,
That squint is rainwater's first cry, little fists retreating.

Bangitoo

Hours of hunting the soft side of a
Fallen treebranch.
The name is only given once
It is torn from you
That cruel heart, a curling of
Mirror mirror
Zhaagwenimo: a little leaf, falling.

That little shell you brought home on top of the leaf-tip,
Trying to name her.
Red-belly up, your tears.

Humming a midnight prelude,
Those dreams that pour midnight and dawn
Rushing waters, your fingers know it.

Breaths are a birthsong. You know your perfection,
Your first breath. Bangitoo, your fingers
Sewed your story long before you inhaled.

Hair Across the Couch

Reading, fingers staining pages.
Her placenta buried, a tree whose name I forgot.

Long legs and hiding your face from the sun
As though the universe might judge you.
The silent daughter with a face full of sky.

Her daddy dead, not knowing her worth, her full
Voice bursting through morning coffees,
Sleepless nights, a room with cat piss and garage sale
Curtains.

Aakwaasige'aw giizis.
So bright. Your heart is a message in a bottle,
Your hands a sign of lost treaties,
A reckoning that sounds like a first breath.

Kindness, a first running, the mare, watching and
Breathing, watching and breathing.

Hair and sun tangled in the treescape.

The Swallowing / Gondon

boodawe

The tsunami of your smile, eyes
Her laugh, centuries, her body a long
Enclaved side, a face so pulling,
Sand winding, our feet,
The only witness,
   her long back arching.

(The small indent behind your ear, the urge when you
Reach back, your pull, your ancient stories inside me).

Imagine if my skin unfolds your history.
The center, you find me.
The way that Nikomis holds your face,
The Origin, the cavewalls, your breath.

Imagine if the birth of fire kept
Secrets that made her move in her sleep,
Tiny whelps that helped the trees breathe
In and out, her pant so arrogant
Bizaani-ayaa-
A sudden shape of love in the corner.

boodawe.

Sadness, that balcony.

Ledging, firearms all around you
Your voice a slaughter
Every name that was forgotten is
a tattoo
Your body and mind a prison
That only loaf, that lies full-bodied.
      Labia hushing,
The blast of heartbeat.
Rape is a conversation over meatloaf and
Wilted salads.
Men's eyes create a vertebrae of old walls
Of long, flat hands opened on pelvic histories
(redheads have the perfect pussies)
      My brown hair lost in the fist of your hands.
Dripping into morning- that pale sun and
her long mouth
shredding little papers a zig
zagging
silence and keys and the sound
of a tiny hip cracking
those big hands fleshing.

Lost

The sister under that white wing, struggling, cleft of a last breath- I couldn't hear that last pant.

That was all.

There is no reasoning left in this heart-
a butterfly knowing her death is certain.

Lips and promises and hands inside of hands- an unwinding of prophecy.

Shattering everything at once. My heart
is a wing. You ate it. You gnawed the last drippings, you stalled my only flight.

Trying to land to die is a crooked tree branch, breathing a name that only dusk can hear. The way you say midnight. Sounds like a fight- your teeth are
Charcoaled white. I found you beside love's corner, hunched over, begging for me.

The dip of your smile is a curse.

Remember us laughing over the rolling hurt that brought us to this shoreline. Remember your hand over mine and the sunset that our body singing made that Tuesday. That July before we all died.
The sand creating your smile is that old bloodsucker; you parted my hair before you kissed me- you missed the indent of my knee when I opened for you.

baakise

Yes, the swallowing throat of my name
Before you forgot it-

Wiinzo. All the names. You scream my name, you open my
name, licking your fingers when you drank my memory,
shivering: all the snowing, so dark.

Trees indented- those birds I counted flying into safety
when you choked on my juices. It's too late, find me here.

It's so dark you remind me- I can't see the shape of you,
those curls of night are your hair- your wounding.

You pulled my clothes off and the swallowed snow
melting, Pine trees, and scentings a thrust, slivers, songs
pressing her faces and mine. zhingobiiwaatig.

I can't see you I can't see you- I'm being eaten- windigo
trails flailing.

The treetops bending
Their limbs offering herself
face lit up and arms opened wide.

Booni. Her garden, petals catching
this open, emptied body.

Thinking it was nikomis or nibi before
I saw you for the last time. booni. Your opening so
splintered- creaking, tiptoeing around and around,

a sanctuary of lies: debwewin's lost
sister. You eat that wing like a promise.

Home / Apike

giiwewedoon

Pink house in the middle of Garden River Reserve.

gidaan. gidaan.

Rustling- legs running toward the house, Nokomis and a pot; Sound of a spoon against metal, over and over. Black hair and neck humming.

Old country music playing Merle Haggard trying to sing through a cracked radio. (the green green grass of home.) Children running everywhere.

Long flowered dress, back- turned, humming to herself. low voice- stirring soup, a long spoon mixing.

My Grandmother sitting in the middle of the kitchen. Soup, feet bare- the floor shaking, cousins everywhere. Aunties kicking us out- basement full of scalded rabbits, and hanging moose staring us down. Touching their bodies, weeping for their emptied eyes, dreaming names that they never knew they had.

Our braids are a monument in the middle of history, weaving centuries together. trees shaking, hugging themselves: the scampering of a thousand little feet.

Memory has no conscience when it knocks on the door, a nightie a mile long yawning, midnight's blanket, crooked curtains mocking.

Mama, nightmares aren't real are they? Her hands in mine. Pull the flap open. Think that you are opening the sky: a low fancy dance like thunder just starting.

That bush that knows our names. A memory of soup, dirt paths, jeeps and skidoos, dead daddies, uncles, cousins and sisters; mothers with a smile that should have been a sculpture; dreams awake in our guts.

Grandma: Soup is ready. Gidaan.

soup
streaming down our chins- chickens arguing with our ankles.
memory is a punch to the throat.

Mikwendan
Remember.

Old trees that remind us that we are theirs.
Bakwadaabidebizh.

Yellow pain, growling.
The man panting, his hands shoving his forehead too hard.

His mouth spread open like a map.

The tooth came out,
They cheered.

They pulled him down the hallway by his feet while he heard drum sounds inside of a sky so black, no stars, no trees- no brothers to save him.

That long trail of blood
Mopped up quickly with
Yesterday's shoe marks.

Everything Reminds Me of You

My baby's feet pickpocketing my heart-
Your heart was under hers.
Your restless sleeping, the
The way you turn to your skeleton
To think, praying down a sky
That you are unsure of.

You walk like a free man,
A slight bump that only
One behind you can see-

But your eyes have bars
That only the moon recognizes.

Turmeric, ginger, the wanting on
Your breath, that kiss that
Can slay a thousand warriors
At once.
A tea left cold where your hand left it.

I saved the memory of your night sounds
The same way I packed my
Baby things once they grew-
I used my heart like a little
Box to keep things remembered.

A heaving pulse when I wake up
To you gone. Another ghost dream
Where you are holding me,
That smile that reminds me of
Chasing my father's love
That smile that can enter me
The same way that a family
Can be slain in the night.

These memories are stairs.

A memory of climbing into the stars
If you walk far enough, or falling,
Quickly the world is making you
Remember the fear of heights.

You are the sandcastle I
Couldn't finish.

You are that first drawing that I
Forgot to name.

Every song threads your colours
Into me, winding me round and round
Like I think identity built her name
On the art that your face
Makes my memory crave.

You are my open canyon.

Darkness

Darkness like a fishnet
Weaving it not even thinking of the fish-
Remembering the callous laying of the sky instead.

Her hurt ripping the net of your Neck
That you can't reach.

A syllable like a bulbous canyon on your mortuary drumming
That summoning sky and yes you hear it all between the
(oh I hear it) that chapping windy wood song.

Somehow the chasing found a home in me.

Every hurt scabbing so echoed and her voice "I need a bandaid- little bloods dripping- cover it- cover it."

Ishkode: you cover her you cover her you never find her ishkode you cover darkness, your arms blinding the sky.

Guilt Is an Oasis for Truth

Four Christmases you sat with bars in your face and you still call her your daughter?

You could have chosen her first. Know that you didn't.
You would have if you heard her heartbeat.

My belly that you hated even when she was there.

You called me fat when I grew her
Sound in me: my body creating hers.
Every day. So so so so tired,
And you didn't ask.

She thrummed. Stretched.
I felt her. I knew her
Sound before I heard her
I was so tired and you never asked.

Your life is a siren- a turnaround- a praying.
A rotation of memory,
So constant, constant.

You can't even see your own face in the mirror. Because the other side is blank.

I will tell you something and don't talk back. If we were in my Anishinaabe land, you'd be gone.

She forgets you. You force her love: you would fuck anyone you can and that energy is a petroglyph of regret. I won't talk to you. You come to me with a regret I don't hear. You are an insect in the walls. You are asbestos. You are the poison. You are the lies that ruin spirits. You are the invisible that we no longer hear.

You are the line that points towards death- and the chaser of every black-tipped sky. You are the voice that no one hears.

A father without a face- a voice that is already dead.

Your name is going to be inscribed on a long grey wall that nobody remembers, where you take breakfast from a lineup like sunrise.

An echo that we all will walk over as if it never happened. A forgotten refrain, rained over, your memory didn't press hard enough.

He Was Never Here

I talked to him and reasoned a
Heart, watching the fading,
Scathing voices,
Pulling the cords out of
That busy love.

You think I can forgive? These
Signals are a canyon - that
Responsibility for falling.
bargaining his watching down,
Like a neat braid, he pulls up
And heaves again.

There is no safety net.

And you grab my hair- twisted in your palm, panting,
trying to turn my head so you can make contact with your
own sad eyes
You think they are mine, but they are
Yours.

Your last thrust is the goodbye.

The bottom earth sees all those thoughts- you think about
lips you will never have. And you highlight these strangers
who will never love you and
The barrage is a hurt-song
That takes shape
Over and over,
A rocking chair
Without your body in it.

I'm not the same.
Neither are you.

You rove with different eyes and you
Rename yourself and take the hands of coffined soldiers.

Every lonely ignition is your key.

Sweatlodge

Uneven shards of light, and begging for more, her hand gentling the sides of my neck so I can see one pinpoint. I want to leave, I want out. So hot and I'm so guilty and I know that promises are a long trail, nothing but a coyote's laugh, and she's crying beside me, her whimpers are my babies sitting up in the night, neck sounds and needy and desperate and it scares me.

So hard to breathe. The dirt is my promise that the earth still exists- strawberry juice staining my teeth and I swallow the dirt. I can read this what is heat and the darkness and memories that are a Wolf on my back, a Sasquatch, a story that I need to forget. She's crying and I'm afraid. That humming in my ears is too loud, and all I want is to get out, to stop it all, to crawl, become a snake and slither out. My head against the thick canvas, my hair a knot that I'm winding through, my hands clawing at myself, the ground, feeling feeling feeling and I can't feel anymore. I don't want to. I'm afraid.

Nokomis. Her words were water, she'd hum and stir soup, she'd salt the soup so thickly. Her back was our moon and she'd talk to the soup so quietly in words we didn't know. Slippers and those long flowery nighties. The tiny brown wood table with puffy yellow chairs. Aunties rushing in and out, so many of them, laughing, laughing.

I felt like running running running running running and never stopping. And I want to rip open the sweat and crawl out panting. So scared of the heat, the way it reminds me of home, like I'm running through the back trails and running towards the water. It feels like I've never been home. Did I dream my childhood? I wonder if I was even there. I sit up and dream that house alive again. My mother my daddy my sisters, the cats, the dirt driveway, wood stove, the way we all walked on the same floor that is gone. It disappeared- I feel like a ghost.

Rocks and watering promises.

My hand begging for air, her arms inside my hair- tracing my tattoos with her tearing- don't make me feel. Don't make me feel, don't: dont.

The wolfing my throat sound- I remember.

Scaring strawberry nectar I'm crawling out, the blood of my body and the hummingbirds so panting at the sky.

wiikwaji'o.

Arms Soldiering

A sleeping guise
Snores are a monument
You turn to me, your arms a
Mountain gauging an opening
Your breathing a doorway
To those words you wash away
For another day.

Disrupted pillows and you never find me,
hindsight a curse to come home to.

You danced once and you thought it might have been me.
Eight years old and your arms holding a girl.

You love like a sniper,
You kiss like war's playground,
And you make memory a burial
Ground.

Your arms are an anchor
Pulling me up a tethered rope
Splinters and kisses and
Outnumbered hope
Our background song.

Lichen Skin

Like my skin
Sin im in
Like them skins
Lie im in
Lie in skins
Licking screens
Lying schemes
Lie in screams
Likened sheen

Lietchenstein

Dream of Lost Graveyard

I found it first. That old pit of bones filling up the underside of my sledding hill. I put them one by one behind the sick old tree that no one remembers except for me.

I didn't even have to hide them because no one noticed that I was gone. I could sit there and make names for each one of them- maybe put the cedar down for beds- build simple blueprints for a log cabin in my mind.

A crooked skeleton of bones that I knew were family somehow. I put every bone together as best I knew how, and I laid the others down until their ancestors came.

I was sixteen and I wasn't afraid to be alone anymore because you are here. I knew how to put you together.
I laid beside you and I talked to you.

From all of the bones I made the structure of your face- your jawline and cheekbones- the lacrimal being brushed off- that small piece that was stuck alone underdirt. Then the zygomatic- your ghost breath my pillow, long sky endless blanketing.

Beside you I slept the sleep of the dead.

Gichi-noonde-nibaayaan gaa-izhi-gawishimoyaan wii-nibaayaan.

www.ingramcontent.com/pod-product-compliance
Lightning Source LLC
Chambersburg PA
CBHW061751070526
44585CB00025B/2866